The Guide To Directing

&

Filmmaking

For Absolute Beginners

DEDICATED TO YOU, THE READER & FUTURE DIRECTOR

Table of Contents

Introduction

Part One
The Budget
The Script
Casting & Costumes
Location

Part Two
Directing & Filming

Part Three
Rough Cut
Reshoots
Main Editing
Music

Epilogue

Introduction

"I film quite a bit of footage. then edit. Changes before your eyes, things you can do and things you can't. My attitude is always let it keep rolling."
-Terrence Malick

Go for it. Just go for it. Many of you are reading this book because you deciding whether or not you should start a career as a director. In my four years of filmmaking, I learned a few things. And after your done reading this book you're going to know everything I know about filmmaking. Starting from camera angles, writing scripts, editing, and etc. I started directing because it was the one thing I could go all out in. If I wanted a giant meteorite with twenty tentacles, I would put it in. But you can't just put them in, you have to work for it, you have to develop the character and learn how to edit the character. As you might've thought by now, directing isn't always going to be fun. I definitely hit rock bottom at some point and you may think that you're never going to be able to succeed. But when that time comes it's your choice to get back up, and it's your will. My passion for filmmaking started right after I watched *"Singing in the Rain."* I was about nine years old at that time and I was inspired by how well it was shot, the choreography, the visual effects, the practical effects. It sparked a small fire inside of me, but as even I predicted that spark had faded out in time that was my first big mistake. I should have never let that fire die. Soon after I watched one of the best movies of all time *"Jurassic Park."* It was a whole new genre for me, and that finally made me start to make films. I started by making lego stop-motion films, I started to voice act and etc. I had started to learn various tricks about filmmaking. When I was about eleven I released my first live-action movie, *"The Flash Generations."* It wasn't my proudest movie. But it was my first, the following year I had studied more about editing, but I had not studied about filmmaking and directing. My second mistake, I had focused too much about making my movie look 'cool' that I had completely ignored the fact that I needed a good story. So I uploaded *"The Flash Generations 2: The Reversal Return"* to YouTube. Both had a fair share of views but they both shared multiple flaws. Lack of character development, lousy writing, and etc. The following year I had begun to develop *"The Flash Generations 3: Darkseid War,"* I had promised myself that I would learn from my mistakes. I spent eight months writing the script. I had continued to improve it until it was perfect. Of course, a few details had to be removed while filming but I was happy with the final cut. And now I'm going to teach you what I learned from all these years of filming so you don't make the same mistakes I did. Enjoy.

Part-One
Pre-Production

The Budget

"Don't wait around for someone else to tell your story. Do it yourself by whatever means necessary."
—Lena Dunham

In a budget there are two sections:
- Above-The-Line Costs: The most important things that you need to start production. Like the script, the cats, the director, producer, screenwriter, etc.
- Below-The-Line Costs: Things related to physical production. Like set construction, props, furniture, studio rental, etc.

When you make a budget be sure to try to save money. The studio will probably give you the maximum amount of money to use. Be thoughtful and start to add elements that you absolutely need to finish the film before you start to add other elements. The first thing to do is to get the Above-The-Line costs ready. Get the cast, the script, the director, the producer, the legal rights, the screenwriters. And then start to move on to the Below-The-Line costs. Although Below-The-Line costs are very important for production. It's good to make sure you get the Above-The-Line costs all sorted out before moving on. But you have to sort out the Budget before even beginning anything. Without the budget you could use way more than the studio gives you. And you could even run the studio into debt. So be mindful, The budget is the most important part in filmmaking.

THE SCRIPT

"There are a million ideas in a world of stories. Humans are storytelling animals. Everything's a story, everyone's got stories, we're perceiving stories, we're interested in stories. So to me, the big nut to crack is to how to tell a story, what's the right way to tell a particular story."
-RICHARD LINKLATER

A script always has 4 main parts

- **Scene Heading:** A short description of the location and time of day of a scene, also known as a "slug line." For example:

  EXT. WOODEN HUT- DAY

  would denote that the action takes place outside a wooden cabin during daylight hours.

- **Action:** The moving pictures we see on screen. Also, the direction is given by a director indicating that filming begins.
- **Character name:** When any character speaks, his or her name appears on the line preceding the dialogue. In screenplays, the name is tabbed to a location that is roughly in the center of the

line. In playwriting, typically the name is centered, but with the advent of screenwriting software that automatically positions the character name correctly, it has become acceptable to use a similar format for character names in stageplays.
- **Dialogue:** What the Character says
- **Parenthetical:** The action that the character does. (normally in parenthesis)

A film always has three acts:
- Act 1: Where the problem takes action
- Act 2: Where the problem begins to grow and become deeper
- Act 3: The events reach their climax and then the solution.

A poorly written script always dies on Act 2. Usually, Act 2 will be two to three times larger than Act 1 and 3. But with a poorly written script, it can feel like Act 2 never ends. A script should always have these three key subjects.
1. Show what the character wants not who he is. (If the character doesn't have anything he wants he's probably cluttering up your script and you don't need him)
2. A character wants/needs something

3. Something or someone is preventing the character from achieving this
4. The character must do the last thing he ever wants to do to acquire this thing.

For example, a church pastor's daughter runs away from home, he has to find her but it turns out that she had joined a rock concert. And the only way to find her is to join a rock band himself. One page of a script should be one minute of a film. The absolute worst thing a screenwriter can do is show or tell the reader or viewer something they already know. I learned most of my screenwriting skills from *Aaron Sorkin, Neil Landau, and Matthew Frederick.* They said that the last fifteen minutes of a movie are the most important but the first 15 pages of a script are the most important. If you have an absolutely brilliant fifteen pages of a script a studio executive will definitely forgive the 'ok' pages that follow. It'll definitely have to be rewritten but if those fifteen pages really hook the reader they will definitely be interested. When you write a script add every single sound that the actor will make, like hiccups, coughs, burps, etc. These words are the only things separating your script from a book or novel. Write like your writing music, when two or more actors are talking write two or more columns of dialogue, two make sure that the reader knows that they're talking at the same time. If you encounter any problems in your script always go back to the character's 'goal'. One of the biggest problems screenwriters have is that they'll get so caught up in writing the journey that they forget to develop their goal. Even if you see the most complex movies, you can break them down to their most simple state. For example *"Inception"* that's one of the most complex movies but you can still break it down to a simple subject. 'A group of people wants to penetrate a person's dreams up to where they can change his personality without them knowing it.' That's it, but if your movie can't be broken down to the very simplest subject it needs revising. Think "What does my character want? Is there anything preventing him from achieving it? If so what is he doing to overcome this thing?" If you have that broken down subject of your script then you have a foundation that most scripts don't have. What's odd is that it sounds very simple and it is simple but it's actually fairly hard. Every Good movie can be explained in one sentence.

- A group of superpowered people tries to stop an alien invasion. (The Avengers)
- A boy is left alone and it's his job to defend his house from robbers. (Home Alone)

'Jean-Luc Godard' once said, *"A film should have a beginning, a middle, and an end, but not necessarily in that order."* Don't be afraid to start late, and you actually should start late. A movie should start as late as possible. For example:

(Mike enters the room)
(He sees Angelina pointing a gun at him)
Mike: Woah. Angelina put down the gun
Angelina: You should never have come
Angelina pulls the trigger

Look at this script, how could we improve it. Simply by starting late. Cut out everything until Angelina says "You should never have come". Now read it again and then imagine it in a movie. Starting late makes the movie more mysterious and makes the viewer wonder what happened for it to get to this point. And what going to happen next. Always write in the present tense. Unlike a novel, a script will never have the words in future tense while describing an action. Every scene must reveal new information, otherwise, you don't need it. Set a deadline for the protagonist to achieve his goal. And if he doesn't set up consequences that the protagonist would rather die than face. Good writing is always good rewriting, don't be afraid of rewriting or removing some scenes from the script. It could save your movie. The audience should never have trouble keeping track of the characters. If they do try to use more distinct names or give them unique habits. Always assume that the audience will forget details. When A story gets concluded don't let the protagonist return to the normal life they had. Limit their options so they remain trapped in problems and doubt. And their only way out is to go deeper. When you finish writing always read it aloud. Either to yourself or to a group of people. Criticism is always a good thing. A free screenwriting software that will make it easier for you to screenwriter would be Celtx.

Casting & Costumes

"A person's clothes make up part of his character. I draw the character with his costume. I suggest it to the stylists with my drawings; the drawings translate some of my emotional impressions. For me, elegance happens when there is a correspondence between a person's personality and how she dresses herself. Finally, don't forget that costumes, like dreams, are symbolic communication. Dreams teach us that a language for everything exists — for every object, every color worn, every clothing detail. Hence, costumes provide an aesthetic objectification that helps to tell the character's story."

—Federico Fellini

When you start to actually decide which actor you want you have to choose wisely. If you're making a movie based on a book, then see the description in the book. If you're still not sure to try to take advice from the fans. They know more than anyone about the book. But you have to choose someone who is fit and is able to do the role. And also when you are writing the script try to imagine the character. And draw some sketches. See if the character fits right with his costume. If not ask yourself "What does this costume mean to the story? What does it mean to the character? Why this costume?" When all of those questions are answered is when you have yourself a good costume that fits the character and the story. But sometimes all those questions might not be answered. Than that costume is just there for show and it means nothing to the story. In that case, you should try to think of something that would resemble the character more. And means something to the story.

Location

"I always scout locations first. The apartments, the railway tracks, the café, the canal — I figure out the geography of the film."
—Claire Denis

Location is KEY! In a horror movie, there's always that eerie and scary house or neighborhood where all the horror goes on in. In a war movie, there's always that one battle site that defines the movie. Depending on your movie genre you will have to choose different locations to shoot your movie. But before you choose your location always ask yourself. "What does this location have to do with the story? What will this character do in this location? Why does he have to do it in this location? What does this location mean to the character? How will I film in this location? Do I have enough room?" Always think negatively, If you think more negatively that you'll find more problems and solutions to fix those problems. But as I said the locations you choose will become one of the key elements to define your movie. So choose wisely. Also think creatively. If you want a graveyard but there aren't any available at the time being, remember a backyard can be turned into a graveyard a field can be turned into a war zone. There are so many alternative solutions if you think carefully. When you shoot in an area with any liquids be precautious. If you can't absolutely guarantee that you can keep everything safe I suggest that you find an alternative.

Part-Two
Production

Directing + Filming

"The director's job is to know what emotional statement he wants a character to convey in his scene or his line, and to exercise taste and judgment in helping the actor give his best possible performance. By knowing the actor's personality and gauging his strengths and weaknesses a director can help him to overcome specific problems and realize his potential.

But I think this aspect of directing is generally overemphasized. The director's taste and imagination play a much more crucial role in the making of a film. Is it meaningful? Is it believable? Is it interesting? Those are the questions that have to be answered several

—Stanley Kubrick

In filmmaking there are three main stages:
- Pre-production: Everything that happens before the first day of filming like casting, costume designing, budgeting, screenwriting, etc.
- Production: Begins when the cameras start filming and usually ends in about eighty days. After the principal photography is completed
- Post-production: Usually this stage begins before production finishes. When the scenes

are being filmed the editor makes a rough draft of the film. Post Production ends when everything is finished and ready to go.

Start out strong, captivate the audience with a strong image of footage. Something that would make the audience wonder what's going to happen next. In my opinion, directing is one of the hardest jobs in the filmmaking industry. But I cannot stress this enough, you absolutely have to these three things to become a good director.

- Read
- Write
- Watch

These are not should do's these are must do's. You must do these as much as possible. I would highly recommend the movies *"King Arthur: Legend of the Sword, Goonies, Singing in the Rain, Jurassic Park, and Roman Holiday"* They are all such amazing movies and surely they will inspire you. Try to focus more on the choreography and angles in these movies. There are many types of camera angles, some of these may help you.

- The Hero Shot: The Camera angle looking up at the character from a lower point makes the character seem more powerful.

- The Weak Shot: Shot from a higher point looking down at a character making the character seem more powerless and week.
- Change of Focus: A character in focus walking in a blurry crowd makes the character feel like they have an uncertain future. A character in blurry focus walking in a focused crowd gives the impression that the character might be getting his values set straight
- Tilted (Dutch) Angle: A tilted horizon makes an impression that something is not right physically or psychologically.
- Over the Shoulder angle: An angle where the camera is filming behind a character simulating that it is sneaking up on it and that the character is vulnerable.
- Jitter/Hand-held Angle: A shaking angle can project a sense of being overwhelmed and at the center of turmoil.
- The Dialogue Angle: This is where the camera is positioned behind a subject's shoulder and is usually used for filming conversations between two actors. This popular method helps the audience to really be drawn into the conversation and helps to focus in on one speaker at a time.

There are endless more angles that I could spend this whole book explaining but these are the most important. Most filmers and directors tend to ignore the Dialogue angle. But that is one of the most vital parts of a conversation. When you film put your hands up and make your index finger and thumb become a right angle. And then connect your to thumbs together by the tip. This should simulate a cinematic screen. Now see through your hands and decide the angle you want. Make sure that when you film that the scene has humane events like coughing, sneezing, yawning, stuttering. These small actions make your movie more realistic. And follow the script as much as you can. When you film some details will have to be taken out. But try to follow the script as much as you can. And while you film you may start to get dull, start improvising and lose hope. At those times it's good to have one scene from a movie that really drives you forward. For me, it's the final battle scene in *'King Arthur: The Legend of the Sword'* where Arthur fights Vortigern. The choreography is just amazing. Whenever I watch that scene it really sparks up my fire again. Try to find a scene that drives you forward. Also always set up a plan. Be organized set certain times and dates for shooting. So you don't cross your deadline. While directing be loose, let the actors improvise from time to time. Some of the most famous movie scenes were improvised and made the movie a whole lot better. Watch bad movies, sure they may be bad and boring but you can learn what not to do. Keep an eye out for when you started to feel bored, or when you thought it was a bit awkward. In the end, that's what's going to save you, and your movie. Watch closely, become the viewer. Think about where you get bored and if you really need that scene. If a scene doesn't develop anything and doesn't get the character one step forward to his goal then you don't need it. You can always look up to someone as a mentor. But never judge yourself for not being as good as him. Because he is as good as him but you are as good as you. Stop trying to upgrade to his level, start upgrading for yourself and one day without even knowing it you'll surpass that person. Night Shoots are very difficult, my advice is to shoot at day if you can. But if you are obligated to film at night here are some tips. Use your surroundings as your advantage. Let's say you're having a night shoot in a more rural area. Using lights from street lamps is very unflattering and unsmooth making your footage seem less in quality. I suggest finding a big light that is very smooth. Also, use a faster lens using an f2.8 lens at night may result in your footage being very dark. But when you use 41.8 it seems more professional and a lot of light is visible. Don't look at a movie from just one point of view, Every character has their own story. Every angle will change the ambiance of your movie. Try different angles and different stories, That might teach you and the viewers something precious. Everyone has their story, it's just how they tell it.

"George Lucas" once said "Having lots of options means you have to have a lot more discipline, but it's the same kind of discipline that a painter, a novelist or a composer would have. In a way, working in [digital] is much less frustrating than working in film, but it's not as though it's limitless no matter how you go. The artist will always push the art form until he bumps up against the technology — that's the nature of the artist. Because cinema is such a technological medium, there's a lot of technology to bump into, and I think as more people use digital they're going to find [it has] a lot more limitations. Some of those limitations will be [equivalent to] the limitations they had with the film, and some of those limitations will just be because they've gone so far that they finally bumped into the technological ceiling." You might find a lot of limitations in your line of filmmaking. Even when I started I had more than enough limitations. So I had to write my script and shoot my film within those

limitations. If you do that then your movie will be very crummy and boring. But what I learned was that I shouldn't write and shoot within my limitations. I should write and shoot to my liking and set those expand those limitations as much as I need. If you can't make a man fly? Then learn to make him fly! Observe and take action. The show, don't tell. When a narrator is telling a story try to show the story more, don't show the narrator telling the story show what the narrator is telling. Follow the action, the camera is the eyes of the audience. They want to be as close as possible to the action. Make a good view by moving and zooming in and out at the right time. A flawed character is better than a perfect character. Have the character have annoyances and problems to make him be more interesting. Even if the first shot seems perfect shoot it again. This will help you when you need reshoots. Remember every film is three-dimensional. When a character is talking there will be other sounds in the world also. Birds chirping, car honks, crowds talking. Always think that. *"Suspense doesn't come from speeding things up it comes from speeding things down"* - Neil Landau & Mathew Frederick. In a film there are two things that really create suspense or any other feeling:

- Rhythm: The pattern created by the individual scenes
- Tempo: The Pace of a scene

These two Feelings are what determine the movie genre. Even though a scene is genius or thoughtful, think to yourself. "Is it absolutely necessary to the story? Does it prepare the audience for what comes next? Does it deepen the character?" If you can't answer these it's probably not needed. But don't worry it's okay to shorten a movie. Quality should be a higher priority than quantity. The climax is more than action. It's the moment where the character realizes his/her truth. It's where the character's shame and fear are stripped away to find a better version of himself. After the climax resolves the problem in a fast and satisfying way. Don't tie up all the loose ends leave the audience wanting more. Be paranoid. While filming scenes with foods or liquid always have a double wardrobe. When casting children try to cast twins or triplets. Have two or three replicas of vital props. Avoid expensive scenes that require boats or water. Make sure that animals can perform the desired actions before bringing them in. Save time and money. Shoot non-chronological, If you can't shoot a specific scene at a certain time then move on to another scene. You can always come back. Start early, this will save you time. Recycle locations, a football stadium can become a colosseum. A coffee shop can become a five-star restaurant. While filming directly centering something or someone causes a very uninteresting mood. But by dividing the frame into thirds will give a rough guide for placement. Horizons are usually placed on the lower third of the frame. An actor's eyes are usually placed on the higher third of the frame. Usually, the proximity of face-to-face dialogue is two feet. But on camera, they look too far apart, and viewers will realize the empty void in the middle. Put the actors in uncomfortably close proximity. These days people tend to have a short attention span, but if you hook someone in the first 15 minutes and the last 15 minutes. There's little to no chance they're walking out of the theatre board. Grab their interest and you have them.

Part Three
Post-Production

Rough Cut

"Trust yourself so that the mistakes you make are the ones you've made and not something you've made because you were afraid to do what you wanted to do. Own your mistakes, then you can own your successes. Try to be as good a listener as you are a speaker. Don't just put the emphasis on saying things. Listen. You can learn a lot even by saying no to things. You help define what you do want and what you can do. I would mainly say trust yourself and don't curl up in the fetal position and cry as much as you did."

—Jennifer Lynch

This chapter is all about mistakes. Forget about the visual effect. What your going to do right now is learn how to make the rough cut of your movie. First what you're going to do is put together all the scenes that you shot. Look at your script and put together the movie as the script tells you to. When you're done you should have a very foggy view of how your movie will look like. This is where you see the mistakes of your movie. The little parts where you cut too early when the actors pronounce a word incorrectly. When you find these flawed scenes write them down like this.

Scene 3-Shot 4-Early Cut

This will help you when you do reshoots, which we will touch upon in a little bit. After you've written all these down, write down how you want them to be fixed.

Scene 3-Shot 4-Early Cut

Later Cut

This will help you know how to fix the problem when you reshoot the shot.

Reshoots

"Listen carefully to first criticisms made of your work. Note just what it is about your work that critics don't like — then cultivate it. That's the only part of your work that's individual and worth keeping."
—Jean Cocteau

Reshoots are where we right our wrongs. When you reshoot a shot or scene try to go at it from different angles. Shoot the shot multiple times. So when you go into the main editing you have a variety of angles to choose from. And when you finally find what you're looking for move on. But don't dictate be open to suggestions. Reshoots are the last moments that you can fix your mistakes so if someone suggests something than listen to them. After all, they're moviemakers too.

Main Editing

"Final cut is overrated. Only fools keep insisting on always having the final word. The wise swallow their pride in order to get to the best possible cut."
-Wim Wenders

Most directors would give this burden to actual editors, but in my line of directing, I did everything. And for most homemade/short movie makers they won't be able to afford a professional movie editor. In that case, I would highly recommend *'Hitfilm Express'* for new editors with absolutely no experience. It's very easy to learn with just a few tutorials from YouTube. When you edit it's really great to start from scratch again. Get rid of the rough cut. Start fresh, Put everything together just like you did to the rough cut. But when you start to put all these together you may find some issues here and there and at this point, you can change them. Remember it doesn't have to be like the rough cut. After you've finished putting it all together I recommend that you tweak with the brightness and contrast depending on your movie genre and the ambiance that you want the audience to feel. When you start to tweak with the brightness and contrast don't overload on anything. Having to much black or white can be unpleasing to the viewer's eyes. After that, you should now add the visual-effects. While adding visual-effects don't overdo it. Having too many visual effects can make your movie look unprofessional and make it look like your trying a bit too hard. After that is done adding color correction to each individual scene based on the feeling you want to give them would be the best. Color has a huge impact on one's emotions. But overdoing it can also be very uncomfortable to the viewer's eyes. Just a tint of a color making it barely visible would be enough.

- Red: Anger, passionate, lustful, embarrassment
- Blue: Shyness, Sadness, Calmness
- Yellow: Fear, happiness, cautious
- Green: Disgust, envy, sickness, friendly, or greedy.
- Grey: Depression and emotionless.
- Black: Cold or mournful.
- Pink: Cheerful, embarrassed, and love.
- White: Sick, shocked, scared, cold, and mournful.

Most movies are shot in a wide angle. If you shot on a phone or camera it would most likely come out not as wide as the movies are usually shot. To fix this there are two ways. You can either crop the video to make it wider. Or you can add a letterbox to the video giving it that cinematic wide angle without stretching the video. When you're done with these steps your movie should be ready to go. But there's something missing. Music.

Music

> "Music is, for me, a great tool of a filmmaker, the same way cinematography, the acting, editing, post-production, the costumes are. You know, to help you tell a story."
> **—Spike Lee**

The music that you think will be perfect while filming a scene is never perfect for it. Whether you compose, borrow, or buy music you need to find the best one for the scene. Imagine having a comedic scene but in the background, there was sad music. That wouldn't fit well. Instead, use the right music for the right theme. Also when you add music you need to find the right level of sound. With too much sound, you could muffle out the actor's voice. With too less sound you could make the music seem awkward and seem like its there by mistake. Also before you start adding music be very aware of the copyright laws. When you add music to make sure that it has a smooth and natural enter and exit. Or else it will feel unnatural and unprofessional. When the credits roll let the music naturally continue from the film to the credits. That will give the feeling of satisfaction or the feeling of wanting more. But in the end, the music is the cherry on top. I suggest that you start early and finish the latest you can. That will keep the viewers more hooked in the movie.

Epilogue

"There are no rules in filmmaking. Only sins. And the cardinal sin is dullness."
—Frank Capra

I hope that this book has helped you to realize your goal in filmmaking. But these are only the basics of filmmaking. There are so much more for you to learn. But if you've finished this book it means that you have now begun your journey. If you want to learn more about filmmaking I suggest that you read "101 Things I Learned in Film School" by Neil Landau and Matthew Frederick. *"Cinematography: Theory and Practice"* by Blain Brown. Most of all the things I learned was from these two books, experience, and classes. If there is anything that I haven't taught in this book that you are eager to learn. Feel free to research and write it down on the director's notes below. That will be your book. Good Luck, and Goodbye.

— Gabriel Jung

Director's Notes
By: _____

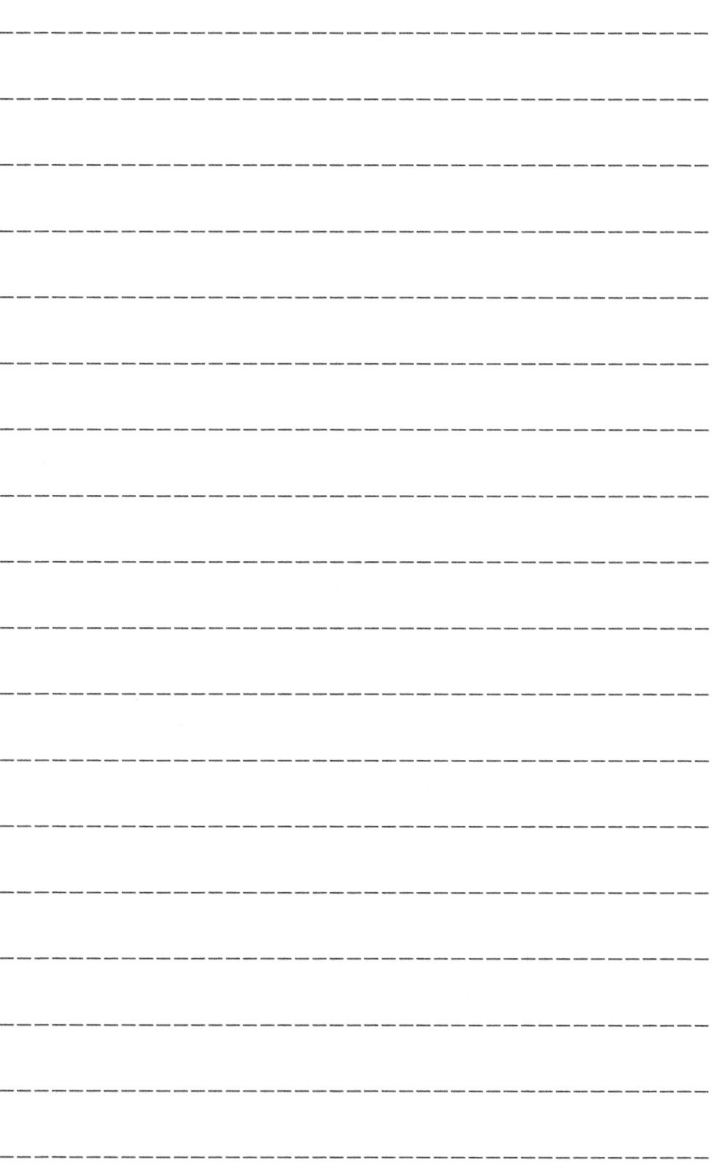

"Whether in success or in failure, I'm proud of every single movie I've directed."

—Steven Spielberg

"Good Luck, and Goodbye"

www.ingramcontent.com/pod-product-compliance
Lightning Source LLC
Chambersburg PA
CBHW030457220526
45464CB00006B/2564